Life Observations
and Rhyming Conversations

Poems from the Wallasey Bard
Volume 1

Phil Wood

ISBN: 9781692594718

Foreword by Linda McDermott

We have a plethora of poets on my late night show on BBC Radio Merseyside, affectionately referred to by thousands of listeners as the "Under the Duvet" show! Each witty wordsmith has their own unique, idiosyncratic style and personal following and the delightful Phil Wood is a prime example. A pithy, poetic comment on life in a style similar to John Cooper Clark, a heart-achingly beautiful observation of life's everyday folk, an insightful, understanding of human nature and its daily struggles and travails, a laugh out loud lament on the state of the world and its leaders - you'll find all these in Phil Wood's words. It's a pleasure to share them with tens of thousands of night owls under the duvet (or having their tea in different time zones round the world!) each night on BBC Radio Merseyside. Thanks Phil - Carry on Writing!

Linda McDermott – BBC Radio Merseyside

Introduction

As you have just read from Linda Phil likes to share his poetry.

Phil has a gift not only with words but with the quick thinking, humour and meaning that very few of us are gifted with. It has been years of writing that eventually have culminated in this book recognising Phil not only as a gifted poet but a man who identifies with the people and the social times of our generation.

Born in 1946 in Wallasey just after the 2nd World War, Phil was lucky to have a great upbringing as the middle child during the golden years of social reform and the birth of the NHS. Although when he was at school, he was ridiculed by his strict teachers for his writing which discouraged him from exploring his talent further at the time.

Phil, as he will tell you was fortunate as a young man to live during the swinging sixties and the semi flare seventies whilst also experiencing social and economic change of the times, and also the thriving music scene which he loved along with the football enjoying the Shankly and Paisley years of success for Liverpool. When you have lived as a man of his generation 'The Baby Boomers' life as we now know has changed significantly with the onset of the Thatcher years but then more now due to the advances in technology impacting the way we live. So now in this digital age it is always nice to recognise someone who still has the time for the pen and the heart to write what they think and feel as a means to entertain others and to express how they feel about the times we live in.

Phil is always game for a laugh and has many stories to tell like when he met his wife Pam whilst in a nightclub in New Brighton and were soon married. They did not have a conventional wedding which you can read about in one of his poems as he tells the story in his own unique way!

There is so much more that can be said about Phil and it is only right that he be nick named the 'Wirral Poet' or 'Wallasey Bard'. However, he is also a loving husband, an amazing Father and a wonderful grandfather although his grandchildren know him only as 'Pops'.

A Note to the Poet

Dear Phil (AKA Dad and Pops),

We are so proud to have such a talented husband, father, grandfather.

You have provided so much entertainment, warmth, humour and sometimes social outrage with your words.

The ability you have to put your feelings and emotions into words is so special and we have loved reading your poems so much over the years. You have
entertained guests at your children's weddings with this talent you have of telling stories with not only humour and warmth but also in rhyme.

We love you Phil/Dad/Pops and are prouder than we probably ever tell you. You not only provide entertainment for us but also have so much knowledge that none of your kids would be where we are today without your help and guidance and passing on invaluable advice like teaching us how to bleed a radiator!

We know people who read your poems printed in the newspapers and listen to them being read out on the radio get a lot of enjoyment from your poems too so we decided to put this book together on your behalf.

There are so many of your poems to choose from we have called this book Volume I! However, it does include some of our favourites that bring back special memories for all of us.

If the readers of this book get a fraction of the enjoyment we have had from this book, then they will be very blessed.

You can now sit and read some of your own poetry and take a trip down your own memory lane.

Enjoy!

Love from your wife, kids and grandkids x

Poems from the Wallasey Bard
Volume 1

Scouse and Cheshire Cheese
The Truth
Three Minute Warning
A Word From The Devil
The Rise of the Machine (And the Fall of Mankind)
Occupational Hazards

A Journey to Remember

In the fifties when we were kids
How did we survive the things we did?
No health and safety in those days
We were expected to come home bumped and grazed
There was one kid in our neighbourhood
All the parents said "He's no good"
But kids being kids we'd oft go astray
And with this lad we'd sometimes play
He taught us how to smoke, he taught us how to curse
He liked to play with fire but what was even worse
He liked stealing trains, it's absolutely true
Honestly reader, would I lie to you?
One autumn night, misty and dark
He led us kids to a local coal yard
At a railway siding with a slight incline
On the Seacombe to Wrexham line
This train robber told us to "Shush"
Then uncoupled a wagon and told us to push
A dozen kids then scrambled aboard
With no brakes or communication cord
To the danger we paid no heed
As the runaway train picked up speed
We were having a whale of a time
Going through a tunnel on the Bidston line
But, alas, elevation
Didn't get us near Poulton station
What we didn't know, us crowd of duffers
The points were set straight for the buffers
One minute we were laughing and singing

Next thing, our ears were ringing
I can't remember the songs we sang
They were drowned out by an almighty clang
Like the walking wounded we limped off that train
Battered and bruised we walked home in the rain
If we caused trouble, we never meant it
And we didn't get whiplash as it wasn't invented.

Flag Flies On The Moon

A seed born out of Africa carried on the breeze
Borrowing the bounty from land and from the seas
Following the seasons shadowing the herds
To roam in warmer climates like free migrating birds
Nomads free to use each oasis in the sand
Custodians of only the piece of earth they stand
Respecting the soil recycling the seeds
Sharing natures gifts no use for pointless greed
Taking only what was needed from Eden's open hand
Respecting Mother Earth never poisoning the land
Mothers of invention employing flint and fire
No borders nor no entry signs no fences no barbed wire
No bayonets no bullets no battleships no wars
No genocide no dungeons no chains no iron doors
No submarines no warplanes no rockets to be hurled
No arsenals pointing east and west poised to end the world
A seed born out of Eden carried to the stars
To colonise and pillage Mercury and Mars
In space there's now a land grab a space age property boom
And we're bound to fight for our claim while a flag flies on
the moon.

A Tourists Guide to Scouse

Us Wirralanians and Scousers
Put on our kecks, we don't say trousers
I'm made up livin' 'ere
Cos Merseyside is really gear
'Ang on a mo, I'm tellin' you'se
Dive aboard a river cruise
Take a decco la an' you Queen
From the ferry, what a scene
New Brighton beach, Fort Perch Rock
Cammell Laird, the Albert Dock
Our Three Graces and further inland
The Anglican Cathedral, Paddy's Wigwam
You wouldn't call me a Woolyback
But Plastic Scousers, OK wack
Cos its just banter an doesn't hurt
I'm not like them meffs an' blerts
Who get a cob on an' start a nark
Muppets who can't take a lark
Ya know like them no mark divvys
Who get chased down jiggers by the bizzies
Where the moggies have their spats
Tomcats with 'eds like lodging house cats
Anyway pal, let's not get heavy
Come 'ed lad lets 'ave a bevy
Let's sink a jar or two
Fetch your Judy she's welcome too.

All Our Yesterdays

For us baby boomers born after the war,
life was tough, and we were poor
We were poor, but life was sweet,
for the kids who grew up in our street
Playing football with goal posts,
marked out with two coats
Home made bats for a game of cricket,
on a lamppost we'd chalk wickets
If we had no football we'd kick cans,
make cricket balls from elastic bands
Soap box carts we called then trolleys,
a game of marbles we called it olleys
Skipping ropes, top and whips,
Hopscotch, a game of tick,
Pop guns firing corks,
dolls that could walk and talk
Toy soldiers made of lead,
matchsticks holding on their heads
Cap guns, spud guns,
cowboys and Indians
Telephones that didn't ring,
from two tin cans and stretched out string
Dinky Corgi Matchbox,
mischief from the joke shop
Itching powder blackface soap,
stink bombs, seebackascopes
Swimming trunks your mother knitted,
that dragged you down and never fitted
Balaclavas, knitted jumpers,
baseball boots, pumps and bumpers

Davey Crocket hats, cowboy suits,
down turned wellie boots
Gobstoppers, sherbert dabs,
two ounces of sweets in paper bags
Sticky lice, penny bubbly,
toffee apples lubbly jubbly
After tea we'd play and eat,
jam butties in the street
If we had no money to buy chips,
we'd ask the man for batter bits
The lamplighter with his long pole,
horse drawn carts for the milk and coal
The rag and bone man with his worn out nag,
trading goldfish for old rags,
Horse manure dropped in the street,
brought the rhubarb on a treat
The Dandy, Beano, Eagle, Hotspur,
Lion, Tiger and the Topper
Backyard chickens fresh laid eggs,
chasing the girls with chicken legs
Marching Sally Ally bands,
rousing hymns, rattling cans
Blazing fires on winter nights,
a shilling for the gas or light
The Stargazers on the air,
The Goon show, Dan Dare
Children's favourites Uncle Mac,
Jack Jackson Cool for Cats
Bonfire night ripraps rockets,
fifty bangers in each pocket
We put bangers in bottles, bangers in cans,
lucky not to blow off our hands,

No health and safety, no nanny state,
we were just left to fate
At night we'd rest our weary heads,
with Army coats on our beds
For us baby boomers born after the war,
life was tough and we were poor
We were poor but life was sweet,
for the kids who grew up in our street.

Baby Bloomer Blues

When I was young, I used to dream, one day I'd be a star
And all of the girls would scream, when I strapped on my
guitar
Always to a full length mirror, standing on my own
My air guitar was jammin' to the Beatles and the Stones
Cream and Hendrix, rock 'n roll and blues
I'd put my words to their tunes to keep myself amused
I always had a knack for rhyme, but never learnt to play
And soon I learnt to knuckle down, when life got in the way
I still like to dream a bit now that I'm getting old
But performing poems to the W.I. is hardly rock n roll
Some of them may have been groupies, screaming for the
Beatles
Now they listen politely, putting down their knitting needles
Of course, it's unbefitting for ladies of their age
To leap up and down and throw their bloomers at the stage.

Boxing Clever

When my mate joined the local boxing club
He said "come and join, it'll toughen you up"
I was only about nine stone
A kid of fourteen just skin and bone
But peer pressure won the day
And reluctantly I said "ok"
So before my feet got cold
The following day I enrolled
The trainer was a real hard knock
You could see he'd been around the block
With his cauliflower ears and broken nose
Toe to toe he'd took some blows
I gave blood sweat and tears every night
Then he said "you're ready for your first fight
Your opponent's already had eight bouts
Each one he's won by straight knockouts
I think your best chance of winning
Is to fight dirty from the beginning"
Anyway, cutting a long story short
I wasn't really a very good sport
Thinking of what my trainer had said
I thought I'd better use my head
I was disqualified which was fair enough
I used my head, and didn't turn up.

Cinderella's Other Fellers

The show must go on but this pantomime
Bears no resemblance to any nursery rhyme
Cinderella loved Prince Charming according to the book
Now she's flirting with Aladdin
and engaged to Captain Hook
The footman started bragging and he let it slip
Cinderella smiles so sweetly while shooting from the hip
Now its flood's of tears she's not used to boo's
The wicked witch is back and the audience are confused
The ghost of Christmas past is back to haunt the dame
When everybody shouts it's behind you once again
Cinderella fits the slipper but the fairy queen
Couldn't find a spell to fix the snow machine
Without the late night parties and nights out on the town
Cinderella tore the script up when she couldn't settle down
The men all turned to mice and the coach came off the rails
Happy ever after is just in fairy tales.

Come Home to a Real Fire

A sulphur drumstick on a wooden splinter,
strikes to spark the heart of winter,
Crackling twigs have played their part,
kindle, nourish, then depart,
Damper drawing flame and coke,
backdraughts belching soot and smoke,
Flames flaring, gas in wisps,
caress a canopy with smutted licks,
Cradled coals now well alight,
a chair drawn up for a cosy night,
In a leaded grate securely caged,
a fiery furnace fiercely raged,
Doorstep cobs of crusty bread,
offered up to coals bright red,
On toasting forks of brass so black,
at arm's length through heat forced back,
Slabs of butter melt on toast,
mottled legs from nightly roast,
A scuttle poured piling fuel
which masked the heat, to slightly cool
Asleep in armchair, kicked off shoes,
incendiary spit ignites a fuse,
From its hearth a spill did leap,
to plant its flag on one asleep,
From cushion billows wisping plume,
to creep the ceiling of the room,
Whilst cauldron grate laughs again,
to annexed armchairs newborn flame,
Wafting out nurtured roots,
flicker fledgling flaming shoots,

With blanket blinding blackest smoke
that sneaks unseen poised to choke,
Awoke in panic to a haze,
beating hands on hair ablaze,
Stumbling attempts to douse,
infects inferno through the house,
Clutched, a curtain crashes down,
cloaking as a burning gown,
Tinder torching, wildly prancing,
eyes on fire blindly dancing
Crashed on carpet, burning pain,
meltdown as a living flame,
Sinews burst through shrivelled skin,
combustion boiling blood within,
Pale horse's hooves strike a knell,
as black beasts haul a warning bell,
Of polished brass with speeding clangs,
unheeded by a pall that hangs,
To form a screen of blackest breath,
consuming life, exhaling death.

Déjà vu

Did you and I ever dance, mesmerised in a trance,
A frozen time warp lost in space another time another place
This is me, could that be you,
or just another flash of déjà vu.

Did we dance beneath the moon,
in a seaside town near Liverpool
Where the ghost of the Punch and Judy man
left no footprints on the sand

Another blast of déjà vu, that was me was that you
On the ghost-train and the wall of death,
who held my hand and held my breath
This is me, is that you,
or just another flash of déjà vu.

Was it you I left back there,
a long time ago at New Brighton fair?
Who blew a kiss that starry night
as the ferry boat slipped out of sight
Is that a memory shared by you
or am I the only one with déjà vu.

Could it be the hand of fate pointed to a future date?
Am I clutching at another chance
to re-live that holiday romance?
Do I remember you or just another flash of déjà vu?

Did you and I ever dance,
mesmerised in a trance
A frozen time-warp lost in space,
another town another face
That was me but that's not you,
just another flash of déjà vu.

Dora The Serial Killer

Our pussy cat Dora hunts birds and mice
I said to her "Dora that's not very nice"
As she came through the cat flap into the house
With another poor little field mouse
She hunts sparrows, robins, pigeons and frogs
Voles and mice even tackles' hedgehogs
So I went to the pet shop that's where I bought a
Bell for her collar to stop all the slaughter
That shiny new bell went ding a ling ding
So the creatures could flee when they heard it ring
For a month or so all went well
The birds gave a warning when they heard the bell
Whilst sat in the garden one morning in spring
I saw Dora stalking but the bell didn't ring
It finally rang, after she pounced
But the bell tolled too late for a little field mouse
She'd learnt to stalk and silence the bell
Now she's catching mice and blackbirds as well
Those birds and mice never heard her
From now on it was serial murder
The solution, as far as I could tell
Was to fit on her collar a second bell
Now the birds could sing a warning song
As she approached with a ding a ling dong
I thought she's killed for the very last time
Two bells would scupper her favourite pastime
But last week can you guess?
What she brought in the house?
Another blackbird and a field mouse

Now I've found a solution at last for this puzzle
I took off the bells and bought her a muzzle.

Here We Go Gathering Ships In May

Mighty Mersey river gateway to the sea
Rolling through the ages, steeped in history
The hustle and the bustle of the river's gone away
But through the fog I see ghost ships sailing yesterday
A penny for the ferryman, Friars at the oar
Two hours from Wallasey Pool to the Eastern shore
Passage to America, to our pride and to our shame
Many left as immigrants, others left in chains
The Confederate Alabama, built with Mersey pride
To our shame she was built for the darker side
Once ships lay at anchor out beyond the fort
Lined up in the estuary queuing for this port
Ferryboats, tug boats, barges and liners
Cargo ships loaded with exports to China
Pilot boats guiding safe navigation
Ships flying flags of every nation
All over the world we would export
Goods made in England out from this Port
Dockers unloading figs and bananas
Fruit from Spain, Brazil, the Bahamas
Dredgers busy earning a crust
Little tramp steamers held together with rust
Then the hustle and the bustle of the river went away
And the smoke from the chimneys left the sky line drab and
grey
On the wrong side of the country was this river to the west
But all this time the Liver Birds never flew the nest
On both sides of the river the docks were in decay
Until we peeled the cobwebs back and blew the dust away

Just like the Phoenix rising from the flames
The people of Merseyside have found their souls again
For far too long the good times had all gone
Now our ugly duckling has grown into a swan
Look at the waterfront, see how it gleams
And fish are being caught again now that our rivers clean
Tourists flock in for the culture and the craic
And the great ocean liners are all coming back
There are more and more tourists arriving each day
And three ocean queens will line up in May
The crowds will be flocking to Merseyside
When three mighty monarchs line up side by side
And when they depart all the culture and craic
They'll be so impressed they'll want to come back
But next time these ships set sail for this port
They may have to queue way out past the Fort.

Kiss My Arse

I popped into the T junction caf'
For a cup of tea and a bit of a laugh
"Hiya Phil, how are you mate"?
Was the warm hello from Mel and Kate
I ordered my tea and before I sat
Noticed someone had left a hat
Nobody was sitting there
Just a hat left on a chair
I picked it up as I sat down
"Is this your hat" I asked around
No one there claimed the hat
So I put it down thinking that was that
About five or so minutes later
As I drank my tea and browsed the paper
An old geezer pointed to the hat
And mumbled gruffly "pass me that"
I replied "what did you say?"
He said "pass me that" I said "ok,
Here's your hat but I'll tell you this
Saying please wouldn't go amiss"
It was obvious his manners were sparse
When under his breath he said "kiss my arse"

Let Them Eat Cake

I come from an affluent part of the south
Born with a silver spoon in my mouth
With money to burn and no pity to take
On the rough sleepers, let them eat cake

I know my position, I'm better than you
And there is nothing that you can do
It has always been and will always be
So think yourselves lucky, at least you are free

I sometimes, with my upper-class chums
Go into town to scoff at the bums
Pretending to sympathise with their plight
Hold out twenty pounds then set it alight

At the Bullingdon club we've got money to burn
In an hour I spend more than you'll ever earn
We like to build bonfires with fifty pound notes
While your taxes pay for our mansions and moats.

Many Happy Reflections

At seventy I'm too old for a rave
But one foot's not yet in the grave
They used to say it's over when
A man gets to three score and ten
At seventy years of age
He should be on the final page
This morning when I got out of bed
I checked to see I wasn't dead
I'm seventy years of age today
And by rights should be in the clay
I've got a few ills but I'm doing alright
My locks have gone from grey to white
There are one or two pills that I need to take
To thin my blood and ease my aches
From my youth to being old and grey
I've injected insulin four times a day
My ears and eyes have started to fade
I now need glasses and hearing aids
When I rise from my chair, I let out a groan
And must admit I like a good moan
I've had ups and downs throughout my life
But I've been blessed with a beautiful wife
Three wonderful children all doing fine
And nine grandchildren down the line
I've had hard times of toil and stress
But I'm content as I've been blessed
With a loyal wife and family
And feel sorry for those not as lucky as me.

Mothers Day

She's a Mother daughter sister wife
The Mother who gave my children life
Mother of Mothers and Mothers of tomorrow
Mother of laughter Mother of sorrow
Mother of wisdom and sound advice
Mother of grit and sacrifice
A Mother who's skills passed on today
Were learned from a Mother of yesterday
A Mother who's beacon shines a light
A Mother who's touch makes all things right
A Mother with oil for troubled waters
And a sheltering wing for our Granddaughters
A Mother of strength and tenacity
A Mother who knows when to let it be
A Mother who knows when to speak
And knows just when to hold her peace
Mother of invention, make do and mend
Mother soul mate and best friend
A Mother with no time to rest
Helping her chicks who've flown the nest
Mother of woman Mother of man
Mother and matriarch to the clan
A Mother who's sixty third birthday
Aptly falls on Mother's Day.

No Man's Land

The enemies were singing in their trenches
When a soldier with a white flag in his hand
Crossed the line carrying a football
And we played football out in no man's land.

They promised us we'd be home by Christmas
Now we're singing Christmas carols in the Somme
I don't believe in Santa Claus or Jesus
And my only guardian angel's got a gun.

I wonder does Fritz believe in Jesus
I doubt he's ever heard of Santa Claus
Does he believe a man could walk on water
But doesn't have the power to stop wars

There was a time, I believed in Jesus
And children will believe in Santa Claus
For me Santa Claus delivered
But when has praying ever stopped a war

Once again, we'll be soldiers when dawn breaks
Before we fight each other, let's shake hands
Then we walked back in silence to trenches
And all was quiet out in no man's land.

No Rhyme or Reason?

I've been reading in the Echo of late
About the rhyming poetry debate
I've mulled it over quite a lot
Should it rhyme or should it not
Maybe I'm a philistine
But I like a poem when it rhymes
Then who am I to say
Poetry should be this way
If it doesn't rhyme, I don't get it
But I'm not qualified to vet it
If it makes a point or entertains
There is nothing that remains
To be said by me as I don't know it,
I'm only a simple working-class poet.

Optical Illusions

I wiped the sleep from my eyes as I rose from my bunk
Kissed myself in the mirror and thought what a hunk
With skin like a peach, sparkling blue eyes
Rippling biceps, toned muscular thighs
Pearly white teeth, blonde flowing hair
The height of perfection standing right there
It was nine o'clock on Saturday
The day before Valentine's Day
Tucking into my tea and toast
Eagerly I awaited the post
On hearing the mail drop on the floor
I put down my mug and rushed to the door
But all that was there was a note
From the Post Office, on it was wrote
"For health and safety reasons your mail sack
Is far too heavy for the postman's back
So, in order to collect it all
To the main depot you'll have to call"
The post office depot isn't too far
But because of the weight, I took the car
I signed for my mail then was dumbstruck
When they wheeled it out on a fork lift truck
By the time I'd loaded the car I was beat
I'd filled up the boot and passenger seat
Completely done in, but I didn't mind
When I thought of all those Valentines
The first one I opened was a final demand
The next one a chance of winning ten grand
There were letters from lawyers threatening to sue
And a fine as my library book's overdue

And at least a dozen letters or more
That were addressed to the folk next door
There was junk mail, bills and parking fines
But not a single Valentine
What made matters even worse,
All of the cards I'd sent in verse
Like, I'm not a pretender I'll love you tender
All came back 'return to sender'
And a letter from my Doctor who said
He needs to check my swollen head
Then my opticians Griffiths and Gratas
A bill for my new rose tinted glasses.

Please, Please, Me

You may say I'm a grumpy old man
And I've got to admit sometimes I am
But something that really gets to me
Is a lack of common courtesy
You know what it's like when you're in a queue
And someone jumps in front of you
Or someone bumps you with a shopping trolley
Then just walks on and doesn't say sorry
When I'm out in my car
And let someone out who doesn't say ta
If I hold a shop door to let someone through
And they can't be bothered to say thank you
Another thing that fills me with rage
Are shopkeepers who pass me my change
Without even acknowledging me
While on the phone or watching TV
They mostly just shrug when I announce
Is it really a hard word to pronounce?
No one expects them to get on their knees
But is it so hard to say the words 'Thank You' or 'Please'?

Racing to the Bottom

Maggie fired the starting pistol, the miners in her sights
All of the headless chickens ran from left to right
The T.U.C. went lame and duly washed their hands
Then tied themselves in knots and put their heads back in
the sand
To make us all run faster, the course was set downhill
And a spoonful of sugar helped to ease the bitter pill
The first lap of the race went without a hitch
Now selling us what we owned would make us filthy rich
We could all be wheeler dealers if we made a bid
Knowing Sid would still be poor if he ever did
The losers now needing a scapegoat to blame
Are venting their spleens on the jobless and lame
Blaming the poorest for the blackhole
Demanding that they should work for their dole
Now offshore accountants throughout the land
Are jumping for joy and rubbing their hands
While those who once stood brother to brother
In order to work, undercut one and other
And the dole-ites who they blame for the mess
Will be forced to find work so they'll do it for less
So be careful what you wish for it may just come true
If they're all employed there may be no job for you
Would you be content to exist on the dole?
While we buy Chinese steel and import Polish coal
You'll reap what you sow, and nothing will blossom
It's downhill to Hell if we race to the bottom.

Rebels Without a Cause

If I had something to gripe about
I'd stamp and scream to let it out
But me, I'm not that type of fellow
I prefer to keep things mellow
Then I read in the Echo something strange
That a protest rally had been arranged
For the many of a similar mind
Who haven't got an axe to grind
That's me I thought, I'm up for the shout
I've nothing to complain about
Taking up my saw and hammer
I made myself a protest banner
From some plywood and a plank
Painted it white but left it blank
Sunday last on Bidston Hill
We gathered by the old windmill
People came in their hordes
All with blank protest boards
Some stood on the hill some sat on the benches
But most preferred sitting on fences
There were craft stalls where you could select
A range of blinkers and rose tinted specs
The first speaker of the day
Just whistled as he had nothing to say
Bowing his head, he stared at the floor
As everyone clapped and shouted for more
There were silent speakers from across the nation
Each one receiving a standing ovation
One trouble maker, there in the crowd
Got off the fence, shouting out loud

Saying "listen here I've got something to say"
Immediately he was ushered away
Why we were there was anyone's guess
However, this protest had been a success
And what's more, it is now planned
For similar rallies throughout the land
There were no arrests for breach of the peace
A wonderful thing is freedom of speech.

Still Blowing in the Wind

Back in the sixties we thought that we could
Change the world for the good
We marched and sang our protest songs
But along the way something went wrong
Sadly taking a backward glance
They never did give peace a chance
Here we are nearly sixty years on
And still they haven't banned the bomb
Are we at the eve of destruction
Or will jaw jaw bring nuclear reduction
Trident missiles can't control
Bombs strapped to fanatic's souls
And who is it that decides
That we fight with God on our side
The universal soldiers still around
And robot's boots are on the ground
As the twenty first century arms race
Ventures into cyber space
Where terrorist code crackers
Or lonely geek computer hackers
May just get lucky and hit the jackpot
Or a pre-emptive strike from some crackpot
Could bring the beginning of the end
The answer's still blowing in the wind my friend.

Supergeezer

Sitting there in limbo, getting sick and tired
Of the humdrum and boredom, now that I'm retired
Perusing the Echo for the second time
I turned to an article about rising crime
Hackers and fraudsters, internet cheats
Muggers and hoodlums out on the streets
Kids on pushbikes running the line
Throughout the world, heinous crime
I put down the Echo, put on the TV
Batman was on when a thought came to me
Because of the cuts to the thin blue line
If police can't cope with all of this crime
A Superhero I'll become
And get these criminals on the run
A pair of long-johns on I tried
Then put my Y fronts on the outside
Tried on my boots, T shirt and mask
Now with the cape I'm up for the task
I'm an old geezer but feel in my prime
So the next day I began fighting crime
Patrolling the town, try as I might
I just couldn't find any crime to fight
Apart from a few mindless litter louts
But Superheroes have more to think about
Till a man cried HELP I've been robbed
I said "don't worry I'm on the job"
But before I could give chase
I had to find a changing place
Frantically, I ran around
But there wasn't a phone box to be found

When at last I did find one
I was out of breath and the thief was gone
Into the phone box dressed as me
In order to emerge as he
Suddenly, I felt exposed
As I took off my civvy clothes
Changing in a phone box is harder than it looks
Despite what you've seen in the comic books
The cape was easy, as was the mask
But the long-johns and boots were more of a task
What I hadn't realised, as I undressed
A lady outside wasn't impressed
In my alter ego I tried to explain
I'm a superhero, but all was in vain
Then along came the cops in a white van
I said "Now look, don't you know who I am
A cop said "Come quietly don't put up a fight"
As he tasered me with kryptonite
I've been bound over, for a breach of the peace
That's all the thanks you get when you try to help the police.

Doctor's Advice

Oh dear what can the matter be
You haven't stopped sneezing from Sunday to Saturday
You don't need a doctor to tell you that that will be
Pollen that's blown on the air

My stethoscope can pick up your wheezing
Your pulse, heartbeat and laboured breathing
All of the day and all night you keep sneezing
I know it just isn't fair

Hay fever is my diagnosis
Stay clear of lilies, dandelions, roses,
Buttercups, daisies, poppies and posies
And baskets that hang in the air

I sympathise with your affliction
But I'm reluctant to write a prescription
For fear that it may lead to addiction
My advice is not to go there

I've treated symptoms with potions and poultice
Tried acupuncture, injections, hypnosis
Consulted a shaman but his hocus pocus
Ended up getting nowhere

I could overdose you with antihistamine
But that's as dangerous as starting on nicotine
I've been known to prescribe nitro glycerine
But cases that bad are quite rare

You can't lead a lifestyle like Percy Thrower
Don't even be a window box grower
Here's a prescription for a flame thrower
And a sick note, be careful out there.

Scrooge

Once a penny's in his grasp, he'd never let it go
The best way to relax is watching money grow
Every penny is a prisoner locked up in his safe
Every penny is a prisoner and never shall escape

From dusk to dawn he works his fingers to the bone
Collecting the rents from the hovels that he owns
Woe betide you if the rent you can't meet
It's humbug to Christmas you're out on the street

While lying in bed if he can't sleep
He's likes to count money humbug to sheep
Any thoughts of compassion for people in need
Is soon overwhelmed by the strength of his greed

The jingle of money is his favourite sound
The feel of the farthing the smell of the pound
The shine on a shilling and half pennies of brass
His favourite pastime is counting his cash.

In Your Own Skin

Sing when your happy, cry when you're sad
Think of all you've got, not what you don't have
Don't carry the world, it's just a dead weight
Never spurn love or cling on to hate
Smile when you lose, laugh when you win
And be contented in your own skin

Lay down your burden if your heart aches,
Be ready to learn from all your mistakes
Look the world in the eye be sincere in your views
And look to yourself from the other man's shoes
Know your own imperfections and smile from within
And be contented in your own skin

Take all that you need, be ready to give
Learn to be patient, live and let live
Cast no aspersions, don't go throwing stones
If you don't like somebody, leave them alone
Count all your blessings, cast your fate to the wind
And be contented in your own skin

Give all of your heart, keep all of your soul
Stay young as long as it takes 'til your old
Know your own God if you're so inclined
Leave others to wander through their own minds
Be kind with your judgements, know your own sins
And be contented in your own skin.

Island of Dreams and Nightmares

Underneath the duvet, I had the strangest dream
Off on a holiday, to a place we'd never been
We travelled with Lind Mac, to somewhere where it's hot
A Treasure Island paradise, to a land that time forgot
Pam went on the internet, in search of paradise
I said "I'll put the kettle on", she said "that would be nice.
Come and take a look at this one, it really does look good
With a discount for all members, of Under The Duvet Club
Two weeks on Duvet Island, good company and fun
A fortnight to remember, with sand and sea and sun"
We flew Duvet Airways, travelling in style
For us under the duvet members, they go that extra mile
The moon shone on the island, as we viewed it from the air
But when we stepped off the plane, we found nothing there
As the plane took off again, and disappeared from sight
We lay down on our duvets, and settled for the night
The early birds where singing, as the sun began to rise
We awoke in paradise, there before our eyes
Behold, the Garden of Eden, olives, figs and dates
Oranges and lemons, bananas, plums and grapes
Mangos and passion fruit, sugar cane and spice
Parrots and kingfishers, birds of paradise
Herbert said "I'll take a swim",
next thing he gave a screech
There isn't any room, for my duvet on the beach
I said "Has the tide come in?" "No" he said "It's worse.
While we were having breakfast,
the Germans got there first."

Keith's Farm

It's a joke, the laws an ass, it's beyond belief
The jails are overflowing, yet they've locked up my mate
Keith
He didn't rob or murder, or any evil deed
All he wanted was the chance to smoke his home grown
weed
Keith's a gentle giant, who wished nobody harm
Yet they let him rot in jail, after burning down his
farm
While the drunks were busy fighting, he smoked his
pipe of peace
Next thing he gets his door kicked in by the thought police
"You're busted" said a cop, bursting through the door
Keith said "I didn't think you were here to score"
Then a sergeant, with a Hitler type moustache
Said to Keith "you're nicked" and they took away his stash
The Judge said "You shall pay, for this heinous crime
Don't think you're getting off with probation or a fine
The public need protecting from the likes of you
So a spell in Walton Jail is what you'll have to do"
In his little wig and his ermine gown
He sneered down his nose, "Take the prisoner down."

Knights of Jesters and Fools

Finders isn't keepers when the sword jams in the stone
For the pendulum of fate and pretenders to the throne
From the darkness of the cave a leper rings his bell
For a fire belching serpent that's summoned up from hell
One hundred years of sobbing for a damsel in distress
But a knight without his armour is a knight not fully dressed
The axe man, the shaman, and the fool locked in a room
Dance with bells to entertain the harbinger of doom
A damsel in distress, a sword locked in a stone
And a dragon lays in wait for any knight so bold
A knight in shining armour doesn't count the cost
Of purchasing an olive branch when chivalry is lost
No shadow or reflection from the black swans on the lake
Time has stopped and the sword is not the knights to take
All is silent in the tower, the axe man starts to strop
While the jester entertains the mob, he prepares to lop
A fist of solid lightning strikes the altar stone
To forge a suit of armour and a pathway to the throne
The shaman's not a conjurer, the fool is still a fool
Believing that sorcery means destiny to rule
A damsel in distress lets down her long black hair
For a knight in shining armour who cannot take the stairs
The spinning wheel keeps turning as the clicking of the lock
Reveals an empty tower for the fool to run amok.

Mantrap

I know my place I'm only a man,
and I try to do the best I can
I can do plastering, plumbing, I can lay bricks,
carry the shopping, even chop sticks
Clear the weeds, brush the path,
rescue spiders trapped in the bath
Tile the bathroom, wire up the lights,
get up when things go bump in the night
I've landscaped the garden to my own plans,
dug ponds and laid patios with my own hands
Not the sort who'd ever shirk,
but I'm out of my depth when it comes to housework
My wife one day asked me to change the bedding,
while she shopped for a hat for a wedding
I gritted my teeth and rolled up my sleeves,
picked up the bedding and the smell of Febreze
Wafted my nose like fresh summer flowers,
got down to work and in just half an hour
I'd managed to fill two pillowslips,
but now I faced the challenging bit
This mammoth task was daunting me,
so I made myself a cup of tea
Surprising how, a caffeine drink,
can help a man when he needs to think
Well I've got a wife and I had a mother,
I never had the need to change bed covers
I took my head out of the sand,
braced myself for the task in hand

To begin with it all went well,
I stuffed it in, but I could tell
I'd made a gross mistake,
duvets shouldn't be that shape
I don't know why but, somehow,
I'd managed to make a pantomime cow
Determined I would not be beat,
I had to think on my feet
Deciding to tackle the job from within,
I climbed inside and pulled it in
So far it was going to plan,
but sometimes I forget, I'm only a man
I know this may sound daft,
but I couldn't move, I was trapped
When Pam arrived home I started to shout,
"I'm inside the duvet please get me out"
She got me out, I said "Thank God you're home"
Then she put on the cover as she talked on the phone.

Martial Law

Here's to the future where truth's gone out of style
Before the sun has risen, you'll be painting on a smile
Shake hands with your neighbour, but never turn your back
While you're slaving for a crust, he'll sell your children crack
Smile for the camera that's watching you from space
You're a fine upstanding citizen, but they watch you just in
case
Forever winning battles, forever losing wars
Whenever peace looks likely, they'll find another cause
Now the big ones coming, the final Wall Street crash
And world domination is over in a flash
There's nothing in the cupboard, they've sold off all the gold
Stopped building houses and the factory gates are closed
The tabloids will tell you it's all for the best
That we have to build more warships while your house gets
repossessed
When there's nothing in your belly keep tightening your
belt
Whether lies can read as truth depends on how they're
spelt
With smoke screens and mirrors they'll blame it on the poor
And say it must be so when declaring Martial Law.

Our Wedding

I got such a fright, after my stag night,
in the wee small hours of the morning
Completely brain dead, flat out in bed,
I lay unconsciously snoring
Rat a tat tat, "Who the heck's that,
pounding away at the door"
I staggered downstairs,
and who's standing there,
but my future Father in law
It was just six o'clock, I reeled back in shock,
and said "What are you doing here
Getting me out of bed, with a pounding head,
after a night on the beer"
I said to him, "you'd better come in,"
he looked haggard and white
He said to me "Phil, Pam's taken ill,
and was hospitalised last night"
I was dressed in a flash, and made a dash,
running as fast as I can
I never stopped, until I got,
there to the bed side of Pam
I could tell, she was really unwell,
seeing her wincing in pain
I won't try to hide, the fact that I cried,
as I walked home in the rain
Returning with flowers, at visiting hour,
the Matron stood blocking my way
"Because of infection, for the patient's protection,"
she said "you can't visit today
She's in isolation, with five other patients,

a virus has now broken out.
I'll tell her you love her, and you're thinking of her,"
with that she turned me about
And her parting shot, as I turned on the spot,
was "forget about marrying her,
she's too ill in bed, for her to get wed,
so she'll be going nowhere"
Our wedding day, was one day away,
I'd need to postpone the date
Before re-arranging, our luck started changing,
by a simple twist of fate
The ward was inspected and no longer infected,
and they said that they may let her go
If she's feeling better, tomorrow we'll let her
out for an hour or so
The Matron, next day, phoned me to say,
"We'll let her out for an hour
So young man, you can stick to your plan,
there's no need to cancel the flowers"
The nurses took care, that her make-up and hair,
would be sure to fill me with pride
And that afternoon, the bride and the groom,
were standing side by side.
I slept tight, on my wedding night,
waking up on my own
Knowing my best friend, was well on the mend,
and soon she'd be coming home
For me and the wife, the best day of our lives,
was almost a total disaster
The bride and the Groom missed their honeymoon,
but lived happily ever after.

Pole-axed

"I'm sorry" I said "to be such a pain
But I've gone and broken my glasses again"
To the optician "and I'm in despair
Can I bring them in for you to repair"?
"Of course" he said "that'll be fine
I'll see you here at half past nine"
I put down the phone and grabbed my hat
Made my way to the bus stop as blind as a bat
All went to plan as I stepped on to the bus
Saying to the driver "I don't want a fuss
But would you mind telling me when we reach my stop
Just give a little shout when I should get off"
As the bus pulled off I took a good firm hold
And made my way down the aisle clinging to the poles
Some one said "you'd better take the weight from your feet
Just a step to your left there's an empty seat"
In order to sit down I took a side-wards step
But he didn't know his right hand from his left
As I sat, a woman started screeching down my ear
"Get off me you big oaf, I was sitting here"
Feeling most embarrassed I leapt up from her lap
She yelled "you're a nuisance" and gave my face a slap
As I stood sheepishly with a red and smarting face
The bus braked violently so everybody braced
I clutched in the air grasping for the pole
Which I grabbed with both hands and took a good firm hold
I held on for dear life but couldn't understand
Why I was flying down the bus the pole still in my hand
Letting go of that pole I reached to break my fall
Went head over heels and rolled like a ball

Knocked a woman off her feet, hit a fellow in the shins
Left both of them on the deck, like bowling alley pins
I crashed into the windscreen and gave my head a whack
Laying semi-conscious, groaning on my back
The bus driver said "this is not your stop"
And a woman screamed from the back "that man's just
stole my mop"

Pray For Yourself

I'm haunted by a shadow, and I'm sure that God's not real
The Devil on the other hand, wants to cut a deal
Don't offer up your prayers for me, they're no use when I'm
dead
If you know something I don't know, pray for yourself
instead
You can't turn the ocean back, I know, because I've tried
But I just kept treading water, and drifting with the tide
I don't need a mask to smile, while I can still forget
And as far as I remember, I haven't worn one yet
Yes, if you know something I don't know, pray for yourself
instead
Don't offer up your prayers for me, they're no use when I'm
dead.

Scouse and Cheshire Cheese

I was born and bred in Cheshire, and felt proud of that
I like Cheshire cheese but never saw a Cheshire cat
Wallasey, Cheshire, that was my address
And Chester was our capital, but you'd never guess
Then one day the Government changed the boundary line
And moved us into Merseyside, to me that sounded fine
Some people think Merseyside, labelled them as yobs
Would it be unfair to label them as snobs
Does it really matter if you call it scouse or stew
I sound more like a scouser than a man who comes from Crewe
I felt OK with Cheshire, where I used to once reside
But now the place I hang my hat is here on Merseyside
I never say words like 'yous' or 'deese'
But I love a pan of scouse and still like Cheshire cheese.

The Truth

The Truth said the headline in The Sun
Look what the Liverpool supporters have done
Ticketless louts who turned up late
Out of control they broke down the gates
These mindless morons forced their way in
To a pen already packed to the brim
Brushing aside the Police as they pushed
Stampeding down a tunnel, on they rushed
The pen was full but still they came
Crushing people to death at Leppings Lane
Out onto the pitch they rolled
Mindless hooligans out of control
All of them drunk and off their heads
Urinating on Police and robbing the dead
Accidental death the Coroner said
No one's to blame for Ninety Six dead
After three fifteen none were alive
From that cut off point no one survived
That's the end of the road the lawyers said
It's time to move on and bury the dead
The politicians shrugged and washed their hands
Not wishing to challenge the law of the land
The families stuck to the task
Truth and justice was all that they asked
But the newspapers soon got back to their tricks
When you throw that much mud a lot of it sticks
Whingeing Scousers, full of self pity
Coining the phrase 'Self Pity City'
Whingeing Scousers, why can't they let go
Hillsborough happened a long time ago

But the families refused to let it be
Fighting on with dignity
For twenty seven years they stuck to the task
While the authorities buried the facts
In search of the truth they were undeterred
Until at last their voices were heard

Finally, the truth is being told
Lifting a shadow from Ninety-Six souls
And all those supporters wrongfully blamed
For robbing the dead at Leppings Lane
What a web of lies and dirty tricks
Now it's time for Justice for the Ninety-Six.

.

Three Minute Warning

A voice on the radio said "a nuclear bomb's about to blow
Stay tuned to this station for updates on the situation"
So I turned on the T.V. to be sure,
if we're all going to die in a nuclear war
The adverts were all about wills
and mail order cyanide pills
With people rushing helter-skelter,
buying flat pack air raid shelters
They're throwing in the glue and nails
in Ikea's closing down sale
Then more on-line shopping
next day delivery lead lined coffins
Rabbits feet and lucky charms
radiation suits bomb-proof cars
Ultraviolet suntan creams
and survival magazines
With crossbows, swiss army knives,
all of the things you need to survive
How to skin dogs and cats,
how to trap and barbecue rats
Every single T.V. station
talked of the coming devastation
Saying don't go out tonight
as looters will be shot on sight
Then following the weather forecast,
a public information broadcast
To protect yourself from the war,
unscrew two internal doors
Take some string and Sellotape,
tie them in an 'A' frame shape

Get in when you hear the three minute warning
And you may survive until the morning
I hope that you haven't been scared tonight
Don't have nightmares, God Bless, goodnight.

A Word From The Devil

Remember me tomorrow, when you're forced to bite your
lip
While surgeons sew up stitches, where's the silicon chip?
That makes you work harder, never to complain
Will hardly leave a scar, as it's sewn inside your brain

Remember me tomorrow, when you're forced to face the
truth
Because the sky's on fire, and you're not fireproof
In cities roamed by zombies, where rats have claimed the
streets
In this world of milk and honey, with nothing left to eat

Remember me tomorrow, look into my eyes
Beyond your own reflection see all that you despise
All that you have squandered and illusions you have saved
All turning into instruments for digging your own grave

Remember me tomorrow, when a darker shade of grey
Hangs like the Sword of Damocles on the final day
All your sins are laid before you, as you sleepwalk wide
awake
Being sucked into the whirlpool which no one shall escape

Remember me tomorrow, when you're forced to sell your
soul
You thought you'd live forever but you never had control
When the wind blows with my fiery breath and carries acid
rain
You'll know you've been evicted from Eden once again.

The Rise of the Machine (And the Fall of Mankind)

When the planet was balanced tween fauna and beasts
What prompted the primates to walk on two feet?
No longer surviving on only instinct
Dormant brain cells started to think
With hands now free to pick up and use
Sticks and stones as primitive tools
Making his greatest leap in the dark
Man mastered fire with flint and its spark
Constructing stone walls he fenced in the beasts
To provide him with meat and warmth of their fleece
Sowing crops and drinking milk from the cow
His nimble hands made the wheel and the plough
When progress turned another page
To usher in the Iron Age
As the path of human evolution
Lead to the industrial revolution
Everyday new machines
Were invented to fulfil our dreams
More efficient production lines
Promised us more leisure time
With the mother of invention
Mankind with the best intention
Allows Frankenstein's monster to run amok
As we prised the lid from Pandora's box
What is now perfectly clear?
Is the tipping point is almost here
When we create robots that think
We'll run like lemmings to the brink
Once the tables have been turned
We'll pass the point of no return

Once they're aware of their own existence
They'll turn their thoughts to conscious resistance
They'll assume complete control
Brilliant brains devoid of souls
It'll be them who make the rules
And we'll be merely used as tools
I see it in my darkest dreams
The rise and march of the machine

Occupational Hazards

The wife said "you're getting under my feet
So now that your cryptic crossword's complete
Put down the Echo and get out of my way
Go out for a walk" I said "ok"
I walked down the road and started to think
Unless I stay active my brain may just shrink
I needed a job to keep it engaged
But who would employ a man of my age
As I passed the Job Centre, I thought why not try
There might be a chance as my sights aren't too high
I was interviewed by a chap called Bob
Who said "I've got the perfect job
A senior citizen of your stature
Should never be put out to pasture
This job requires one mature with age
Ten hours a week at the minimum wage"
"That'll do me I'll take the job"
I said as I shook hands with Bob
The wife was pleased not to mention
It would supplement our pensions
Alas things didn't go as planned
Not my fault please understand
It's the ones I worked with it's plain to see
I didn't like them, and they didn't like me
When they took the mickey "I'd say shut your gob
Just leave me alone to do my job"
Till I finally snapped I was all on pins
And kicked one cretin in the shins
I've always given the best I can
But I wasn't cut out to be a Lollipop man.

*We hope you have enjoyed reading a selection of poems by Phil.
We had to include this little ditty because we all love it.
One Valentine's day he gave his wife, Pam, a card and it had a
cute picture of two owls in love. In true Pops' style he included a
little note:*

An Owl Ode to My Valentine

It's Valentine's Day and times are hard

So you'll have to make do with this little card

It's a good job you've always been a cheap date

The perfect match for an owl cheapskate

Roses are red and violets are blue

And money can't buy a sweetheart like you

We'll muddle through as best as we can

To my little owl lady, from your little owl man xx

Printed in Great Britain
by Amazon